# A DOLL FOR THROWING

# A DOLL FOR THROWING

*Poems*

## Mary Jo Bang

GRAYWOLF PRESS

This publication is made possible, in part, by the voters of Minnesota through a Minnesota State Arts Board Operating Support grant, thanks to a legislative appropriation from the arts and cultural heritage fund, and a grant from the Wells Fargo Foundation. Significant support has also been provided by the Lannan Foundation, Target, the McKnight Foundation, the Amazon Literary Partnership, and other generous contributions from foundations, corporations, and individuals. To these organizations and individuals we offer our heartfelt thanks.

Published by Graywolf Press
250 Third Avenue North, Suite 600
Minneapolis, Minnesota 55401

www.graywolfpress.org

Published in the United States of America

ISBN 978-1-55597-781-8

2 4 6 8 9 7 5 3 1
First Graywolf Printing, 2017

Library of Congress Control Number: 2016951417

Cover design: Jeenee Lee Design

# CONTENTS

3    *A MODEL OF A MACHINE*

4    *OF MANNEQUINS AND BUILDING EXTERIORS*

5    *SELF-PORTRAIT AS A PHOTOGRAPH OF A PLATTER*

6    *SELF-PORTRAIT WITH OTHERS*

7    *THE CHESS SET ON A TABLE BETWEEN TWO CHAIRS*

8    *ONE GLASS NEGATIVE*

9    *DWELLING IN OUR TIME*

10    *TWO NUDES*

11    *STILL LIFE WITH GLASSES*

12    *ON THE BALCONY OF THE BUILDING*

13    *THE MIRROR*

14    *ADMISSION*

15    *NEWS OF THE DAY*

16    *A NUMBERED GRAPH THAT SHOWS HOW EACH PART OF THE BODY WOULD FIT INTO A CHAIR*

17    *THE HUMAN FIGURE IN A DRESS*

18    *THE SILK AND VELVET CAFÉ*

19    *OUR GAME. OUR PARTY. OUR WORK.*

20    *PORTRAIT IN THE FORM OF EPHEMERA*

21    *PHOTOGRAPH PRINTED WITH HATCH-MARKS OR LINES ACROSS THE PORTRAIT*

22  *SELF-PORTRAIT IN THE BATHROOM MIRROR*

23  *IN THE GARDEN BEHIND THE MASTER'S HOUSE*

24  *IN THIS PHOTOGRAPH I AM UNTITLED*

25  *THE DOLL SONG*

26  *STAIRWAY, SEASIDE*

27  *THE GAME OF ROLES*

28  *FRAGMENT OF A BRIDE*

29  *GESTURE DANCE DIAGRAM*

30  *IN THE STREET*

31  *THE HEAD OF A DANCER*

32  *THE TRANSFORMATION ANXIETY DREAM*

33  *THE BRACELET*

34  *A BALLET BASED ON THE NUMBER THREE*

35  *THE SHATTERED MARRIAGE*

36  *ME, A CHRONICLE*

37  *THE POSSESSIVE FORM*

38  *THE ILLUSION OF PHYSICALITY*

39  *THE SCURRYING WHITE MICE DISAPPEAR*

40  *THINGS TO COME*

41  *YOU HAVE TO BE UNCOMPROMISING AS YOU PASS THROUGH*

42  *SHE HE AT THE FLOWER BASKET*

43  *LONG-EXPOSURE PHOTOGRAPH OF A MAN*

44  *PORTRAIT AS SELF-PORTRAIT*

45  *LAST NAME FIRST FIRST NAME LAST*

46  *THE PHOTOGRAPHER, BERLIN*

47  *THE NEW OBJECTIVITY*

48  *THE ICON IN THE HANDS OF THE ENEMY*

49  *ONE PHOTOGRAPH OF A ROOFTOP*

51  *MASTERS' HOUSES*

52  *TOMB IN THREE PARTS*

53  *THE EXPRESSION OF EMOTIONS*

54  *MASK PHOTO*

56  *AN ANATOMICAL STUDY*

57  *THE MISSING NEGATIVES*

58  *IN NOVEMBER WE INCHED CLOSER*

59  *HAVING BOTH THE PRESENT AND FUTURE IN MIND*

63  *AFTERWORD*

65  *A NOTE ON LUCIA MOHOLY*

67  *NOTES*

75  *ACKNOWLEDGMENTS*

***László Moholy-Nagy***

Artist: Lucia Moholy (British, born Austria-Hungary, 1894–1989)
Date: 1926
Medium: Gelatin silver print
Classification: Photographs

Between 1923 and 1928, when Moholy-Nagy was a teacher at the Bauhaus in Dessau, Lucia Moholy was one of the most prolific photographers at the school. This portrait was made at the entrance to the "master's house" the two occupied at the Bauhaus.

—The Metropolitan Museum of Art, "The Collection Online"

# A DOLL FOR THROWING

I'll begin by saying that objects can be unintentionally beautiful. Consider the simplicity of three or four self-aligning ball bearings, the economy of a compass. Brilliant, no? We thought so. We had confidence in architecture and design beyond the base commercial. Stage settings, furniture, typography, everything came with a moral mandate. The machine was important, of course. At four o'clock in the morning ideas came effortlessly, as if out of the air, the way a teapot or a pan comes cleanly out of the cupboard. In the blank space between the following day and the previous night, you see the beauty of a propeller, for instance, and think, yes, I want that silver metal to mean something more than just flight.

Living looks random and barren and formless when you're adamantly busy inventing a *now*. The past will subtract itself from the new, especially wherever glass is a clean element on the edge of the no-longer-ornamented eave.

I'm a double of myself, one half a doll that was spared, one half dead. A feather is a form of frou-frou and only so interesting. We want no more of that business. We are spent. Some. *Mit freundlichen Grüßen.*

At the end of the day I never close my eyes. The landscape just is. What good is sighing. There are lines in her face that don't yet exist. The doll's face is breaking, she has no wrist.

## SELF-PORTRAIT AS A PHOTOGRAPH OF A PLATTER

A platter can embody a wish to be simple. We are who we are. *Wir sind.* I also speak English. I married a master. I taught him something. I know what I'm doing. An image stands for the thing that is taken. I am taking everything I see. This is how I see myself. The platter is very flat and somewhat lasting. You or I might even say I made it last. Circum/ambient: as more or less to be around.

Before I moved out, there were five of us: me, my sister, my mother, my brother, and the man who modeled what we were all to think. He said we are nature, like it or not. Sun, clouds, rain, and reeds like those monks used to show their humility back in the Middle Ages. I wonder whether humility gets in the way of ambition? I wanted to travel. The morning my mother said I mustn't, I wanted to stop her mouth and shake her. It felt like taking a step.

I wanted to be my father: leave, return, leave again saying nothing to no one. My mother: a musician. An orchestra of self-absorption. My brother: a filmmaker who says he wants to reinvent himself. He thinks an American name will make a new man of him. As if a pill dissolved sublingually can make the mouth speak in a manner the mind never knew. We are in a café. The mosaic ceiling above us is a blue overturned bowlful of goldfish. Each open mouth is a blind spot. Want. Want. Want. I catch sight of myself in a mirror.

We were ridiculous—me, with my high jinks and hat. Him, with his boredom and drink. I look back now and see buildings so thick that the life I thought I was making then is nothing but interlocking angles and above them, that blot of gray sky I sometimes saw. Underneath is the edge of what wasn't known then. When I would go. When I would come back. What I would be when. I was hard working but sometimes being becomes a habit: I came on stage wearing a lavender fitted dress with a stand-up collar. He looked at me, he took a drink. A man examining a hothouse flower. I clicked, then closed my eyes—the better to imagine my upcoming absence.

Knife to the narrative root, a pillow over the aperture opening, the café narrowing to silk and a single view. With a velvet curtain over your eyes you drink the ink from an open orbit. The glass lens asks you to answer: say yes for one, no for not now but maybe later. The marble maybes scatter. The bear lumbers off. Did you know what I meant when I said, Do you want someone to love you, or just this? I too am still. I refuse to ask mother may I, may I, may I, only to be given another maybe.

## TWO NUDES

I was working in a bookstore and as an antidote to the twin torment of exhaustion and boredom, one day I went with a friend on a walking tour. We made it as far as Berlin and there I met the man I would move with to a boarding house, then to furnished rooms in the flat of a civil servant, and from there one morning in January to the Registry to be married. We then moved to a studio apartment and two years later from there to where boys returning from the war would remove their collars and sew them back on with red thread to demonstrate the end of their allegiance to the cruel and fastidious past. Everyone wanted to be launched into a place from which you could look back and ask whether the red was also meant to enact spilled blood. You could say so, but only if you want to insist that history's minutia is best read as allegory. The fact is, history didn't exist then. Every day was a twenty-four-hour standstill on a bridge from which we discretely looked into the distance, hoping to catch sight of the future. It's near where you're standing now. One day we were lying in the sun dressed in nothing but our skin when a camera came by and devoured us.

In the east-west dialogue between objects—i.e., *chose* and things and the many-colored costumes inspired by them—there are only two players: history and pictures. Each one creates images that will go on to exist in the imagination. Signs and signifiers can be subtle or not, subtext or top layer. The sweetly said *doux* includes the unstated question "Do you x?" Whether by design or not, the portal opens either way wide or narrow; the latter is the tailor's eye which knows by sight both the home coming queen and the needle's prick. When sewn together, one can be both bridge between and the lover embraced. Or does one thing insist each is one or the other? East or west, the repurposed steel becomes the semblance of a body and bodies are romantically eroticized line-&-figure simplifiers the way glass will always be *en verre en* France and at the same time *shiro* can be a Japanese castle covered with white snow and a white porcelain dish decorated with a Snow White scene and/or a watch-crystal smokescreen over a long-night chrysanthemum sun.

## ON THE BALCONY OF THE BUILDING

There's no sleeping now. No morphia dream-pact with night as a needle. We are staying awake and pressing against one another as if whatever is left is all that will ever be. We need one another as if one were on a fragile bough being sawed. I see the trace of a faint scar embedded above your right eyebrow. I knew then what it was to feel. The dying fall.

# THE MIRROR

My hair is held back by a barrette, the tree in the background is green. Out of sight, birds talking on the right, to the far left and almost too far off to be heard, a dialogue between two men. I wish I could break in two and be formless, one half listening in, one half thinking about nothing but the fact that the nape of my neck is too warm. The express train flashes past, followed by a crashing silence. I've rejected the milk-mild smile. It's married to the risk of fossilization. Granite with blood in its veins is still granite. On the bark of the pine behind me, a single cicada is glittering. That world is an island where it is always morning and the cool breeze is always invigorating. You can tell by my hair, how it's blown back. You can tell by the light. It's there and not going anywhere. There is no moment that isn't all spectacle. The theatrical silence is the sun. The gray stage is winter. The circle is pure dilation: the shock mouth of me looking back at an avalanche of broken glass.

# ADMISSION

My mother was glamorous in a way I knew I never would be. Velvet belt buckle. Mascara lash. Miniature crimson lipstick alive in the pocket of a purse. Her bow mouth was forever being twinned to a tissue. I never would wear that black windowpane see-through blouse, mother-of-pearl buttons tracing the path down her spine. Every woman was her rival. You could say, seriousness made me impossible, exactly the same way beauty made her. I understand men. Some like to have one woman in their arms, while a second one stands on a half-shell, both continuously shifting between being and being seen. Even as a child, I understood there were erotic fishhooks that one couldn't see. I learned to use a camera to see what I could be.

Everything not in was out and we were the bride and groom in the marriage of this ridiculous day and life is only ever a comic opera. To write lower-case after decades of elevating the noun, this could be seen as an arm sweeping the past from the pedestal into the ashcan. To pull a question out of that hat, the one with an electric rabbit hidden inside, can become a critique if the overreaching world looking in is terribly nervous—like a diva sitting in a warm-water bath extolling the benefits of hot running water. *How embarrassing*, the singing chorus says above a clatter of cubicles where the press corps pushes out kitsch and vulgarity. Perhaps the staged hot bath *is* an embarrassment but who doesn't want to forget the tank blocking the main street as well as every other exit. The news of each day is that time passes quickly regardless—some hours, however, are longer than others, with many more minutes that count.

## A NUMBERED GRAPH THAT SHOWS HOW EACH PART OF THE BODY WOULD FIT INTO A CHAIR

I was born awake and knowing and time keeps proving this: men have reasons for breaking the rules. For me, thinking has always been a logical process of if this, then that. I fit into a chair. I sit in a room. I split in two—my body behaves but my mind resists. It's a simple truth that one can occupy two places at one time while sitting in a chair—the same way a poseable doll can be divided from her dress. It's also true that time will mesh us together. Until then, there's another city on the other side of this wall. A list listing reordered details might read like this: light, glass, a metal stairway, one woman sitting on the sill of a window, me in a chair. My feet on the floor, face forward, arm bent, the very best of the body tucked into place. But we are not dolls. We feel. We make mistakes.

Naked or not, I'm a costume that moves, figurine with a face that changes. You could call me a mood. I begin cheerful but sometimes turn solemn when confronted with my own mythology (wolf in a cape, cat-claw scratch on a cupboard door, mouse tail in the hand of a bland farmer's wife, a drop of blood on her shoe). Today's beginning ended in a dream. In a fantastical bed, a lover leaned in to kiss me just as I realized I was part machine, part primitive urge. I left the bed and said, You know, don't you, not everyone is so disposed. And then I heard from inside my head, You should say, not everyone is so disposed to your utopia. Only then did I realize I'd been inexact. Even here there are scolds that tell you how to be. Sometimes they live inside. Naked or not, I am trying to tuck my arms invisibly behind my back so that all you can see are my breasts and my highly simplified head.

Come over here, she said. It was the façade
no self can be without.

A fire can be hot flame and black carbon contagion that ends in a smoldering that goes on emitting smoke and warming whatever is near. It was like that in the years when we moved from one place to another. Some say a war ends only when it becomes smoke rising from a book in a library destroyed by fire. And yet that fire sparks another. That library moves to another city and then to another. And so, war, not once but over and over. And everywhere, there are those who care and those who don't. When metal and glass were becoming a building, the wealthy came in cars to gawk while the workers arrived on foot. Both brought deep scowls and the belief that if only the past would outlast today, they could be what they had never been, day after day eternally happy. They said without saying that what we were building must be destroyed.

Three items in an envelope. A photograph of two, four, six, eight, nine boys boarding a bus. Not boys, men. Dressed in the long wool coat of winter. Something "based on the life of." What can a moment outlast? That question becomes a theory, theorem, mechanism. Three boys, one girl, a tree brushing back air off her forehead. Paper, six clean sheets, a monogrammed envelope. An index. The physical bias to existence becomes some wedge, the inexact value of an empire of ether. Tick-tick. The amphibian emerges from water, walks off stage. It's as if evolution is embodied in absence. Someone is lying on her back. She turns over. Her breath is in the air. Or in the idea of atmosphere.

## PHOTOGRAPH PRINTED WITH HATCH-MARKS OR LINES ACROSS THE PORTRAIT

Some photographs invent a method of fiction, an illogical trying to think differently history. The true aim of archives is:

a complex, relating, narrating voice and rare versions of what happened, actuality of actuality. This requires a plastic mind. Archives of photographs create a direct category linked to the culture of written history, along with the premise of what may have happened, spread over the course of images that exist in two different temporal dimensions, i.e. when the photo was made and when we see it.

These opposed logics disfigure the true act—the incidental fact that this did exist—morphing the two times into one simultaneous reality where temporality remains to say this: what did exist may still exist. I think the living know this or else will come to know it when they look at this photograph.

# SELF-PORTRAIT IN THE BATHROOM MIRROR

Some days, everything is a machine, by which I mean remove any outer covering, and you will most likely find component parts: cogs and wheels that whirr just like an artificial heart, a girl in a red cap redacting the sky, fish that look like blimps and fish-like blimps, an indifferent lighthouse that sweeps the horizon. I wasn't a child for long and after I wasn't, I was something else. I was this. And that. A blast furnace, a steel maze inside, the low-level engine room of an ocean liner. My eye repeats horizontally what I by this time already know: there is no turning back to be someone I might have been. Now there will only ever be multiples of me.

Does the erotic exist outside architecture? The shepherd asleep, the shepherd awake—his staff in his hand. Sweet are the fields of. Exiled from home am. A sandwich of tendered lamb. Overhead, stars marvel in a heaven of now. As soon as we have a building, we have a mash-up of the dystopic present and the future that will not sit still. A is for agitation. B is for building a house. What does it mean to be a master? To have mastery. One woman, one man. Who is whom. Self-interest as an imperative is unlike any other. Where does one live? It's early in the history of coupling. No one is more alone.

And seen through. The way a wine glass placed on a table transparently suggests wine will be served. I don't mean to say that is all that I am but it is a fact that even in the dark, angles often conduct the eye into a lighted interior. There, someone sees and says to herself, I wasn't always this way. One sometimes becomes.

A stage set, curtain, window, wall, the shape in a shadow drawing the eye into the dark. In time you see she's a she who has moved from the edge to the desk to elsewhere. Simply said, the absence at the desk edge equals her presence stage left. Both ghosts. This is more than a question of dimension.

When a well-lit bamboo lattice expands, it can morph into Madame Butterfly. On an enlargement of the still, you see a lake shape on the upper right, the realm of nature. You've seen this opera before. There's a ship on the lake, a god in the house. A man is going away. The woman is here to stay. We all want her to be more than just a lovable glass-eyed facsimile, a robot going through the motions.

One act is loosely based on a love of diamonds. In that act the woman is almost headless and completely naked, a line drawing of her would place her next to nothing.

The fur isn't fake, nor is the lost look. She looks back over her shoulder but keeps the eye bright. A veil should hint at what's under it. The lips are a bow, the present a present. With a spool of thread, she's Ariadne in charge of a labyrinth. On a bivalve shell, she's a goddess. Now a blurred bride on a bed. She is what you want her to be.

A process. A performance. A figural stage. A glass dance where the glass alternates between mirror and see-through. Followed by suspense-filled love affairs with others. Actors alive in your own time. The dead too. Why not? They're easy enough to find. You only have to open a book. In this way the animated pregnant beginning gets reanimated over and over. One day you say to yourself, I am light-dark, warm-cold, up-down. After saying it the first time, you repeat it whenever a wave washes over you. What's ideology compared to that? To the held breath and the heart race up two flights of stairs. At the top, you look down as one does on the edge. Of course, not everyday is gray. On a good day you go to the beach.

In any narrative, facts are present or not. One might assume the more facts, the better the constructed history, since facts are meant to reflect what can't be computed by storytelling alone, which is said to be subjective and therefore inaccurate. In many cases, the story is filled with complex details, which only one person knows. You sit at a table and turn a page on which marks make letters that suggest a timeline. It's clear that you believe nothing will ever outrank your cold and unforgiving erudition, however, everything you think is based, even at the most basic neuronal level, on the way you connect a long line of dots. Refined interpretation requires that you know that someone once said the offspring of reality and illusion is only a staggering confusion. Keep in mind that your mind is a twice-shattered light bulb and on the other side of detachment is the fact that someone is busy living while you are translating the fact that she's dead. Also remember that behind your glass mask is only your mind.

Relative to status and state, one often finds the strategic depiction of an implicated myth: man v. god, fire, female, followed by a beeline drawn to the end of the garden. Outside, the concrete sky and a clamor that might be described as a deafening mechanical distraction, the basic rhythm of which has been set in advance to match a harsh song that goes like this: *metalwork-always-outlives-fabric.* That mess of a crumpled net dress at the bottom of a wardrobe might be a refusal to accept the notion that possibility is something one puts on to go out: a woman for example could still wear the dress but where would she go looking like that? It would be an error to describe her as someone who doesn't know how she is supposed to act, when in actual fact she is acting. Her eyes are open and she is acting like someone looking into a box of scattered catastrophes, saying to the man next to her, "Look at these. Which one would you like?"

In other words, a Caligari cabinet arranged like
a stage, where an invisible hand sets the figures
in motion. You're free to add sound if you want
some. Form, color, style isn't added to but
naturally is. What stage set isn't jagged? One
pale gray silhouette moves toward an exit that's
lit with a light Diderot called English red. It's late
so let's all go to bed. We're young and some of
us won't last. Although who can say what when
is or where why? Please don't tell me tomorrow
is already over.

## IN THE STREET

Here we are, on top of the utopian arc. The water is shallow. An oil spill shimmers on the surface like a lens catches light and folds it in front of a mirror. If someone stands next to you, they are there, even when outside the picture. Which makes total obscurity relative to luck and such. Unlike the law, architecture lasts. A façade, like an ideal, can be oppressive unless balanced by a balcony on which you can stand and call down to those in the street: Come over here and look up at us. Aren't we exactly what you wanted to believe in?

The days when you lean your head forward, then pull your head back, to see the sun is only a chrysanthemum, the eye is a white lake with a black boat moored at a particle pier that says what you want back isn't coming. The white speck says there is a light source that shines day and night far from a balcony on which an audience waits to see us open our doll eyes and close them again. I keep my face facing front to see every last thing that is coming. What is coming is this: a hat to be worn when taking a train, a compact in a pocket, a letter in a pocket, two hands, a waterfall pouring its contents into a well-worn shuddering mind. I'm as devoted to knowing as the dim fish swimming in an ever-widening circle. Today outraced the latest hour of midnight, my hat tells you that. That and that I strangely resemble you: eyes, nose, lips that refuse to open, knowing the face is glass and that glass can make or break you. The dog in the street pauses just as a car comes. Where does it stop? And now this, someone says. The precise line draws the bone that holds the cheek in place. The cheek waits to be kissed by air as it was once kissed by the dark-haired boy in the boathouse whose late-night lesson was that the distance between what had been described and what was now happening was immeasurable. The morning after, the black shoes on the shelf were married to a new all-encompassing idea: the dress is no longer the thing the future is founded on. You put it on. You take it off.

You've three sets of hands but you still can't catch the ball. If the distance were closer, you could fence it in. On a whim, add something thin, a giraffe or two. Have a small zoo. But your eyes won't work. You clown face. Amphibian fingers. A shape moves and finds your forehead. A bare-bulb bright idea. A giraffe is too tall. An okapi perhaps. Your suit is too tight. You're a melting iceberg. Don't make that face. Hear no, see no, say no. Your tie is too tight. Your eyes are upside down. You tunnel under an avalanche. The snow doesn't own you. What does? The stairs inside the tripling device can't be decoded. The pane of glass flowers, becomes a cloud on its way to becoming amnesia.

## THE BRACELET

It hardly matters but the metallic taste demands your attention. Like a pre-planned sleeve tattoo. Like the wrist wielding a titanium hammer. Like that sick all-day tension headache in the too-hot interrogation room. Like Cleopatra's head lodged firmly in a brush that brushes the dust hour after hour. For a moment, a wedge takes a bite out of the sun and you wear that while you pretend the metal band means what you once wore for what felt like a second is now yours to keep. When the theft is eventually discovered, the trap door opens and drops you in.

## A BALLET BASED ON THE NUMBER THREE

We are three: me, he, and she. I am a pocket, he is a needle, and she is the pinprick that resets the elements. A minor annoyance can come to mean more than a minor irritant if it gives rise to a shift in proportion or to a reduction of value. The record of motion is like a slow dance that ends with someone sitting it out. I'm outside now, having left eye, brain, grid, and graph behind in order to become an auto-self-selection machine that allows a whole person to disappear. I feel the law growing weaker (that's father), and the she (that's mother) no longer the rabbit hole into which one falls and falls and falls.

You perform the ritual and replay the ceremony but still Medusa's head poses a problem. Will it explode? Pass from an ordered geometry into a state of decay? Opinions are sought, scientific and otherwise. The enterprise requires some license, the same as the absurd. Not disorder so much as a solidly soullessly matched set of batteries. Or a bored audience held captive by some terrible unforeseen on-stage disaster.

Shapes that begin as just one solution to a common problem can go on to become an inflexible method. Take for example houses. Once a certain way of arranging walls takes hold, it's difficult to imagine any other. Another example might be locomotion, the method and circular means of moving from one place to another. I was drawn early to the idea of other modes of seeing, especially to photography. Looking back, I see myself entering the living room. I see my father crossing the room to open or close a window. My mother's zigzag pattern of static. My sister, the new century's picture-perfect child. My brother, the new century's self-possessed man. At one point, the idea of rebellion became a unified belief. I left. Can you imagine the impact? Who hasn't felt that in order to breathe, she has to splinter the first self and leave it behind? I constructed a second self. I photographed myself as if I were a building.

In [year], the _____s [plural form of husband's last name] moved to somewhere; it was there she did something. From [year] to [three years later], she was also made [title] at [school name] in [place]. In [year] she left [one country] via [one country] for [one country], and as a [occupation] soon made a name for herself, being compared by some critics to [woman's name]. She also lectured to students at [school name] and [school name], both in [city name], the emphasis being on the [specialized subject within the subject].

A body is a mystery of identity and death. Shrewd, you might say. Also spare. The right arm has something of a pared-down style—brusque, forthright, useful except when it's not.

Take tennis: its sophisticated simplicity. Is the ball over the line? The truth is measurable to within a millimeter. Everyone is hoping. This goes on for years. The beauty of certainty is evident. The succinct repetition becomes rhythmic, the figure a form.

Daylight veils darkness in the depths of the mind. You sometimes catch sight of yourself whenever your body, that blood-filled shadow, collides with the wall behind you.

Inside the apartment is a half-eaten insect. Its proportions match both those of the building and those of my body: small and damaged, a delinquent in this prison I think of as a world that can't ever be contained.

## THE SCURRYING WHITE MICE DISAPPEAR

Where have they gone? The cage door unlocked is left open but that answers nothing. The snow outside will hide them if they are successful in crafting flattened versions of themselves and leave through the space where the high wall ends. This is only the nothing that is. Not a horror, or no more so than any other effacing trace, a novel of one hundred chapters that meanders until it arrives at the end where on the last page the reader sees, strange coincidence, his or her name. Spelled with different letters but still the same name. Closing the cover unmasks the guillotine and kills the mice. This is a well-known structuralist principle.

Night's metal wheel spins under the blackout of war, which says no to a world of want. Friday is through until Saturday's alarm at seven. Work is the only redemption. Not the willful insanity of religion where the light-headed with hunger get down on their knees and beg for a crumb from the ceiling crack. Was sick today. Something eaten. Late last night I dreamed of a building that perfectly matched my adolescent longing. I have been breathing a fine layer of dust until this sudden rain eroded the window and remade the entire material world—watch as the ordinary melts into meaninglessness. The film ticks backward each time I replay the death I failed to forestall. This never blurs.

Although it sometimes seems random, the gawking on the street is not imagined. I see the barriers. They are there by design. Every image of a woman speaks of a theatrical body performing a script, the connector that shoulders when there's a war, and embroiders when there isn't. I can see that they, meaning we, are meant to be objects: small scale, fragile, unassuming. Many men see themselves as having obvious affinities with other famous men. Not only from the same period, that would be banal, but from every period since time began, even Adam, even Eve. They see themselves as being more fascinating lying on a bed than the body lying beside them. She is an everyday animal of ubiquitous fabric sewn together with blue and red thread. A certain system that can act as a cushion at night when things are hard. Make no mistake, she is also, when things work well, an almost fully realized artwork repaying the viewer with attention.

## SHE HE AT THE FLOWER BASKET

A circular mirror of the social order is something like a master with an exclusive club membership until a woman comes through the revolving door. He sees her as an angel of mercy with a braid down her back while she sees herself in the mirror and says I'm on the outside looking in. When she says that, his mouth covers hers and they both sound alike but what she is saying and what he is saying is not the same in and not the same as. The moon can be mistaken for a rabbit from the back when it's both a rabbit and a cat.

One man is many. I never said he left me but he left what he thought I was. Yes, and I too had thoughts that went on over time. Duration extends into the future, wraps around the past. Can anyone avoid saying, I once was? Of course now you have those test-tube babies. Your nuclear transfer animals. My brother was at one point making a film that moved forward while we stood still. Looking isn't always gawking. That requires a degree of stumbling open-mouth wonder. What's wrong with that? If you had seen what I had seen. My brother is reading Kafka. My brother Franz. An incidental doubling. I told you before that I spoke English. Or did I? You know it now. You also should know that I communicate through showing how an object acts on me. I'm either in it or I'm behind it. One or two or more. Will you some day really bring everything back from the brink?

Avoidance of boredom drives the body forward. I sleep. I eat. I enter a lightless room. Existence there is limited to the self and whatever image the eye feeds it. The film canister acts like a bank. The emulsion acts like a layer that lies between what I once saw and what I now think. At the moment, the eye feeds my mind this man. His face floats in a frame. His hand refuses the camera. The wiring that makes him behave is invisible. I light him that way. He is connected to nothing and thus without context: no ring rests on the dresser, no shoes on the shelf, no long coat on a hanger. I keep him alive. I place him in a cage.

[Last name], [first name]. Born [father's surname] in [place], lived there until [date]; moved to [place] in [date]; studied [three subjects] at [school name] in [place]; worked at [occupation] in [city] from [date] to [date], and in [city] from [date] to [date]. Married [name] on [date]; divorced on [date]; worked as [occupation] in [place] from [dates] and in [place] from [dates]; created [what] with [name] in [city] in [date]; established [what] in [city] in [date]; subsequently specialized in [occupation] in [city], [country], [date]. Was [something] in [date]; was [other] in [date]; member of [society], [date].

First name, last name, studied subject, subject, and also subject. Was employed as something by various. Was married to and with him went somewhere when. When the something moved to somewhere in date, she began to do something. In due course she did something, as well as something. Collaboration with him was very close, particularly in the fields of something and something, as well as something. Cf. [book title plus date of publication].

Monday was fluid, so no longer matters. There was food and that is not nothing. An alarm. A doorbell. I'm limiting my thoughts to facts. This may be what the near-dead feel as they enter their special sleep. Tuesday, up at five, dinner at eight. Then I don't know what until Wednesday when I woke. Dinner and the desire for knowledge, which we have come to realize is impossible. As much as I know I know it is nothing other than what I assume. Thursday is over. I am toward and away and each type is a tedium. I am afraid I will board the wrong train. I exit the station I find myself on the street, pure evidence, so the eye says. I'm met by a stream of quotidian detail. This morning was and now day is a train with a window and above it, concrete. Where am I? The weather changes. Warmer. Less gray. Less wet. I'm already here. Is this what it means to accomplish? Thursday was sudden. I walk and I walk. I now wonder what I was thinking.

The orbit begins but won't meet its end. Will I ever arrive at a future? An ocean of place names rolls by like a cart on an incline and nothing to stop it. Can it rest? I continue to be against hunger and terror. My own and that of all others. What is constant? One, a bed, or two, the ticking beside it. Buy a ticket, catch a train, cross a border. Take with you only what you can carry. The eyes of the other are on you. The indicative finger is telling you to come away from the window. It indicates that a room is for looking into, not out of. The sway of terror like a dance band, ratcheting up the drum beat.

To disappear, but not this way, not with the body intact but slowly eroding until it's been hollowed out. A diminishing rain followed by a panicked dash to a border where tanks are backed up. We were busy living in a house and about to step out. Who could have known that the same kiss we were having had just been with death? I watched while a man was taken away. I held onto the view of the closing door and when I turned back to the room, there was the small map of the tea-set table, quotidian, benign, symbol of time. The numbers on the wall clock morphed into dots. We are this now I said to myself inside the terror. The indifference of nature added its weight. After that, I no longer thought of time as a transcript but as an ongoing address to emptiness.

Dawn rains bombs on the rooftop while a legend scrolls under a series: one escaped to Siberia, another, to somewhere else. A silver crystal ball reflects what it catches the way a fish-eye lens does—both bend the edges and flatten the foreground. How can one plan? You have an intention, then the right comes out of hiding and becomes the wrong thing. The wrong time. The worst thing. We had hoped means "then nothing." We admired the architecture, sat in the courtyard and marveled at the look of surprise attached to our faces. Two children bounced a ball back and forth behind a wall. We remained committed to finishing dinner and avoiding death. How is the present now? As difficult? Like a murder trial where one is asked to decide if the defendant is guilty or only appears to have killed someone? Would he be guilty? It must go without saying that there is more than one way to look at a situation. What can you do with a building's collection of angles? We lived among facts. What does order cure? If not cure, at least calms while you look at the roof. Or at a stone boat sinking slowly. Winter etches the glass deck. Is it always possible to find an example of what you didn't do well enough? Don't you think?

A handful of small-scale hours unobserved, the sight of cities razed. The ever-active disaster machine pauses to fix itself. You can never answer the question of whether a single death matters. All those sorrows. Radio signals run through rain. Glass hours lie on their sides. A sand bed dead to the world.

## MASTERS' HOUSES

Architectural is one way of being. A background against which the black trees are more belonging than the white walls and made beds of boredom behind them. Inside, a plate is waiting to be emptied, a rose is giving in. I never wanted to be anything but an eye that was open, city to city to city. Master is craftsman but also a brutal building of history. Bleached femurs in slave chains and trains to where. Razor wire master as monster, the memory of. We began where you began, with the thought that the world was about to be. And it was. And still is.

I remove my heart from its marble casing and grind that shell into glass dust and force the dust and the occupational core into a box barely big enough to hold them and watch while the self-sealing lid sets itself. I then take the contraption to a place to which I doubt I will ever find my way back, even if I wanted to, which I don't. I have zero desire for what has been buried after having been done with like that one that was once. With such rigor and exactitude does the end come and more than once, which is a way of making a statement about the infinite duplicity of a suffocating blanket.

Darwin dreams of orchids while I dream of Darwin
saying mutability isn't always elegant, not like the
cult objects we once loved. The now-past post-
utopian scene is so frayed that the residual sounds
like a disintegration tape. What is missing is what
we were when we were the gorgeous beginning.
Silence can be the gray painted edge of a ship
where the water's nothing takes the shape of the
mind forestalling deciding what to do next. Going
downstairs and out again onto the patio, the movie
of your mind returns you to the dodo, a bird now
only believed in. We believed and that brought us
to the drowning of the ticking clock and to air filling
a well-defined building and years.

## MASK PHOTO

I.

Life as a dressed doll. A graveled path no wider than a balance beam. You come to yourself in a dream where a woman's face is imported from the ancient era. Myth always works like this: all goddesses get dressed out in qualities and roped into whatever arena you choose to believe in. Red Riding Hood is an ingénue; Daphne is featureless, a chaste head inside an oval at the distant end of a tarnished tea strainer, her shining beauty left behind. You sail away to the mountains at midnight with the owl and girl-friend his cat. You pick a self and make it last. Waiting fate takes the form of Ariadne who has secrets. Day and night she whispers at the mouth of the maze. You wish you could kill her, but don't. Her understudy is standing by.

II.

The terrible act of the photograph made more so by the fact that the scene is only volatile dyes bonded in an unstable coupling that becomes a red shoe warped by wearing. There is also the red flowered dress one could wear but instead it becomes the moment of someone staring at a radical departure from the limited real. Perfection, you know, is a matrix best imagined as a picture behind glass. The room's circus performed on the surface makes a viewer want to enter its mimetic mouth and melt. Above you, a sugar cube suspended like a lifelong doubt: you doubt that you can ever love what truly is in front of you. You are left wondering what is behind. When you turn around to see, you only see what you want.

# AN ANATOMICAL STUDY

Now I'm an archivist. Indexer of everywhere I have ever been. Of every moment I stood there and there. Of where I was when I was getting and spending. Coming and going. My seeing is now different from what it once was. White burns my eyes. Orange glares back like a crass plastic pumpkin bright in the last null of night. This must be the way any newborn sees a face facing its face. Color catches and brings two wide eyes into view. The archive is a disguise and disguise is a form of experiment, a mask every bit as radical as an overblown detail or some new extreme perspective. Here I am not myself but still me: hectic tulle and self-timer instead of identity. I'm an interceding nameless other and transforming even as we speak: face, make-up, lace, and cliché overlay. Eyes open, I'm someone else. Eyes closed, I'm a face-shape falling asleep.

# THE MISSING NEGATIVES

In science, design, and architecture, there are no answers for what is entirely positive or negative. There is that ships-parts paradox based on the principle of asking what is anatomy and what is a nerve impulse and how does a doll act as a bioengineered replica of a body. How does an empty interior echo? No, Plutarch, no, under no circumstances is a ship rebuilt from the same wood the same ship. Apply the same principle (then is not now) to anything physical and multiply times two. Those two items will never touch again. Proof of that is the fact that the pout-faced neighbor doesn't speak. He stands for some essential silence that is more than merely decorative. He takes multiple forms, first an elephant, benign but crushing, then a bird as the essence of what it is to be betrayed. The tedium of a pink drink, of closed lips, closed mind, without so much as a dimple of kindness to brighten the day.

In November we inched closer to the ledge over which one only falls once. No traveler returns—or if, then borders will have been withdrawn. There will undoubtedly be a film made later and seen documenting the train as it passes through Germany. The soundtrack will have to include the clatter of knives and twice broken glass. Those on board felt a mystifying sense of time blurring more than the usual. To a person they said it felt like a flash. The train slowed, came to a stop, we got on. The hall was narrow, which made some sense—what hall is wide but the kind that cuts through Versailles? Cabins on either side of an hour: a bed, a curtain, a half-cup of water no more. There's no one to ask where we are or whether we'll ever arrive. No timetable. No dining. No dome car, no well-dressed people legs crossed at the ankles casually pointing at the sight of an avalanche or snow on a mountain. I didn't know where I was going. There was dark at night and day never lasted. Each tunnel was a sightless blind and no soothing singsong birdsong. I no longer hear being German spoken. Those who are left are alive. I am among them quietly holding my breath and hoping time will go back to being. The last I saw of the sky, the moon was a man with moronic orange hair dressed up in a frock coat and collar swearing to serve no one but himself to the duped on his way to his tower.

The split image, a glass box that can be divided in two like a warm-water aquarium with angelfish, some with tails lashing one way, others another. The high-rise windows all masquerading as insect eyes. Inside, a house for a room in which an apple is bitten almost in half. A chair one gets up from. Time can move from the general to the visual particular one piece at a time until you reach the infinitesimal where everything is airborne. Place a grid over that and what you have is a tall building that's been imploded. The roof ripped off, the fixtures removed as scrap for melting. Even copper wire can be stripped of its red rubber cover. What's left will look as if it could be reconstructed, become electric again, but no longer dangerous. Although never again would there be that woman who stood up, walked over to a table, then turned to say, "I was just about to say," to a man in the midst of dissolving. The building like a maze, the individual pieces falling, some forward, some backward, the woman and man collapsing, each becoming a sacrifice to the fact of having been. I'm not saying you can change a shape without forever altering the inside. I'm saying the opposite. I'm saying that in some cases the inside persists until long after it doesn't.

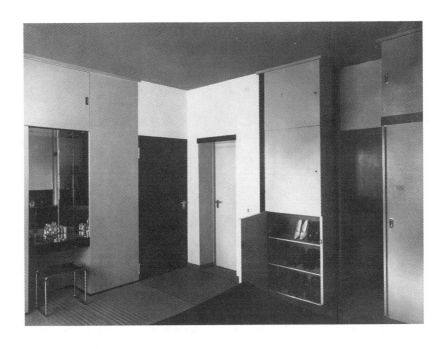

Lucia Moholy, British (born Prague), 1894–1989
*Untitled (Walter and Ilse Gropius's Dressing Room)*, 1926
Silver gelatin print
4½ x 6 in.
Private Collection

## AFTERWORD

The electric brain echoes *Open*, and when it does, only then
do you see how inside the cabinet a row of shoes suggests
that life goes on and on. The unseen hand holding the camera
is modern. The straight lines say so and maintain the illusion
of us looking in from a distance. We are post-then but still
attached. Perception alone can trace the lines between *before*
and *after that*. The shoes in the photograph and their heirs will
soon be buried under *after* and whatever falls from the window
of broken glass that gives onto barbarity. Looking in from now,
the future outside the print's edges includes the unspeakable:
I am what I made. Which also contains, I am out of that which
I made.

A living magician on stage addresses the audience: *I'm
about to pull a rabbit out of an intangible hat.* Out of death. Out
of a row of shoes. Out of a cupboard with a door that swings
open and shut. Out of a doll that is and isn't actual. The doll's
avatar mouth—*we are alike; we are not*—can be made to say
anything: I once lived in London. I once looked across a lake to
where evil planned a "final solution" to the question of envy. I
once tumbled from a balcony, got up and photographed my fall.
I once wrote a book in which my face was inside a frame.

On the potential for error in the present: *Stop me*, the
mouth says, as the dashboard-mind races toward disaster. This
is like saying stop to water in a cup in the middle of a tilt to-
ward an inevitable revision. A drip snakes its way down the fore-
head. That motion was invented to invert what we can't claim
to know about ourselves, much less about another. The nega-
tives are arranged in a circle around us. Lives appear likable
when standing on a balcony, bodies angled toward the empti-
ness below. Below us and them, time continually flips back and
forth between utopian hope and what will be next. The breeze
surrounding the bird-whispers sends indiscriminate messages
to any who listen in on the scattershot hail against a window.

The sill is an unbroken line dividing without from within. That border acts like breath makes time mark the living as over. Imagine yourself inside that room. Can you see yourself? There is a mirror. You think now.

I once read that reading the phrase *a green suede glove* activates a part of the brain that processes texture. Does that mean reading makes it possible to know what it is to feel? What is certain, at least to me, is that patterned marks on paper are a reminder that humans sometimes speak.

In 2012, in a cube-shaped room I saw this—

a Dutch woven textile, hung verso, *circa* 1910 – 1930; Pablo Picasso's *Woman in a Red Hat*, oil-on-canvas, 1934; *Visions in the Night*, oil-on-Masonite by Maybelle Stamper, *circa* 1938–39; a line drawing, *Youth Dismounting*, by the sculptor Marino Marini (a miracle of visual ambiguity: the man, the horse, the merger of two), 1949; a Plexiglas vitrine inside of which were three things: a medicine pot, a "power object," and a figure of a man carved on a staff (Mali), all unattributed, dated *circa* 20th century; an untitled black and white photograph (*Walter and Ilse Gropius's Dressing Room*) by Lucia Moholy, 1926.*

—and thought then about how the objects together brilliantly enacted the democratizing collapse between craft and high art envisioned by Walter Gropius in 1919 and promoted by the vaunted Masters of the Bauhaus movement. The school survived until 1933, the year Hitler was made Chancellor. At that point, the forward-thinking ideas and sleek machine-age style—an elegant form-equals-function—were deemed degenerate by the Nazis. They idealized a past that had never existed except in the form of gingerbread trim. They misunderstood the word *again.* I watched the past unravel and worried about the future.

* Originally taken for a 1926 promotional brochure designed to publicize the Bauhaus buildings in Dessau, it was part of *In the Still Epiphany,* an exhibition curated by Gedi Sibony at the Pulitzer Foundation in St. Louis, Missouri, April 5 –October 27, 2012.

# A NOTE ON LUCIA MOHOLY

She was born Lucia Schulz in Czechoslovakia to an upper-middle-class secular-Jewish family in 1894. The daughter of an architect, she studied art history at the University of Prague. She was fluent in four languages and experienced in darkroom photography. She was working at a bookstore in Hamburg when, on a visit to Berlin in 1920, she was introduced to László Moholy-Nagy. He was a Hungarian Constructivist painter who had also made a few sculptures and some works on paper. She introduced him to photography. When he began to teach at the Bauhaus in 1923, she joined him as a workshop participant in photography. She was asked by Walter Gropius to document the newly constructed buildings in Dessau and the workshop products. Gropius said he was unable to pay her but she would retain the rights to the images, as well as any fees for future reproductions.

She and Moholy-Nagy left the Bauhaus together in 1926 and separated in 1929. In 1933, after Theodor Neubauer, a Communist Party deputy in the *Reichstag*, was arrested in her apartment, she fled the same day, leaving her negatives in the care of Moholy-Nagy. When he left Germany, he gave the negatives to Gropius for safekeeping. Lucia Moholy made her way to France, and then to England, where she worked to secure Neubauer's release. She eventually opened a studio and worked as a portrait photographer, elaborating her ideas about portraiture in her book, *A Hundred Years of Photography 1839–1939* (London: Penguin Books, Ltd. 1939). Her studio was bombed by the Allies in 1945, the same year Neubauer was guillotined in Brandenburg prison.*

The remaining war years were spent working for a microfilm service connected to the British intelligence organization at Bletchley Park. Moholy-Nagy, teaching at the newly reopened Bauhaus school in Chicago, offered her a job teaching photography if she could get a visa; however, her countless visa applications were denied. After the war she began to see the Bauhaus monographs that had been published in the States. She saw that Gropius had used her images repeatedly without attribution in order to establish his name and that of the Bauhaus in America. There are letters sent to Gropius

* Neubauer was interned in the Buchenwald concentration camp from 1933 to 1939; he died in Brandenburg prison on February 5, 1945.

during the war years asking whether he knew where she could find her negatives because she had been invited to give lectures in London about the Bauhaus but couldn't do so without images. He wrote back suggesting she reproduce images from the prints in the pages of old magazines. There are letters sent to lawyers after the war, asking whether she could be compensated after the fact for the negatives' use. There are letters in which she begged Gropius to return her negatives. There is his reply in which he wrote that he needed them, and insisted that she had given him the negatives when she "chose" to leave Berlin. There are prints with her name stamped on the back crossed out and Gropius's added. The letters are in the Bauhaus archives in Berlin and in the Gropius archives at Harvard.

Some half of her glass negatives were eventually returned to her, sent by Gropius C.O.D., in shoddy packaging, with significant loss. In the late 1950s, she was hired to set up a photographic archive and laboratory in Turkey. Eventually, she moved to Switzerland where she worked at a publishing house that specialized in art criticism and art education. In 1983, she published an article titled "The Missing Negatives" in the *British Journal of Photography*, documenting the history of the use of her negatives without attribution—a final effort to close the gap between the work she had made and her ownership of it. She spent the rest of her life exhibiting her work and working to correct historical inaccuracies in books and articles about Moholy-Nagy's early work, much of which had been made by the two of them together in the darkroom. She died in 1989 at the age of 95, outliving most of the other principals of the Bauhaus school and movement. These poems are not about her but were written by someone who knew of her.

## NOTES

*COVER IMAGES:* Four photograms attributed to László Moholy-Nagy: *Laci und Lucia*, 1925; *Untitled* 1925; *Untitled* 1923–24; *Eiffel Tower and Peg Top*, 1928. All four, based on the dates, were likely collaborative images made by Lucia Moholy and László Moholy-Nagy.

*TITLE: A Doll for Throwing:* Alma Siedhoff-Buscher's Bauhaus *Wurfpuppe* (translated variously as throw doll, throwing doll, or doll for throwing) was a flexible and durable woven-yarn doll with a round wooden head—which if thrown, it was said, would always land with grace. A ventriloquist is said to "throw" his or her voice into a doll that rests on the knee.

*A MODEL OF A MACHINE:* Sven Wingquist, *Self-Aligning Ball Bearings,* 1907, and *Outboard Propeller,* 1925, Aluminum Company of America, from *Machine Art* (MoMA Exhibition #34, March 5–April 29, 1934, organized by Philip Johnson).

*OF MANNEQUINS AND BUILDING EXTERIORS:* Getty Research Institute: Inventory of Bauhaus Student Work 1919–1933: photographs, including 2 of mannequins and 2 of building exteriors, ca. 1930.

*SELF-PORTRAIT AS A PHOTOGRAPH OF A PLATTER:* Getty Research Institute: Inventory of Bauhaus Student Work 1919–1933: Hans Finsler, n.d., 1 photograph of a platter of chocolates.

*THE CHESS SET ON A TABLE BETWEEN TWO CHAIRS:* Chess set, 1924, pear wood, natural and stained black, Josef Hartwig designer, manufactured: Bauhaus, Weimar.

*ONE GLASS NEGATIVE:* Getty Research Institute: Inventory of Bauhaus Student Work 1919–1933: Franz Ehrlich, ca. 1928–1932, 1 glass negative titled "Studier arbeit."

*TWO NUDES:* László Moholy-Nagy, photograph of Lucia Moholy and Edith Tschichold, ca. 1925.

*STILL LIFE WITH GLASSES:* Iwao Yamawaki, silver gelatin print, 1930–39.

*ON THE BALCONY OF THE BUILDING:* Umbo (Otto Umbehr) photograph of Hannes Meyer (director of the Bauhaus school from 1928–1930) with student Hilde Reindl on the balcony of the Bauhaus building, 1928,

Bauhaus-Archiv Berlin. Irene Bayer-Hecht, *Bauhaus, Dessau (From a Balcony)*, silver gelatin print, 1925–28, Museum of New Mexico. *Bauhauslers on a balcony of the studio building*, 1931, Stiftung Bauhaus, Dessau.

*THE MIRROR:* László Moholy-Nagy, *Photogram Number 1—The Mirror (Der Spiegel. Fotogram Nr. 1)*, negative 1922–1923; print ca. 1928.

*ADMISSION:* Walter Gropius, "Bauhaus Manifesto and Program" (1919): "Admission: Any person of good repute, without regard to age or sex, whose previous education is deemed adequate by the Council of Masters, will be admitted, as far as space permits."

*NEWS OF THE DAY:* News of the Day *(Neues von Tages)* is a comic opera by Paul Hindesmith (libretto by Marcellus Schiffer), first performed in 1929. It parodies celebrity, marriage, and modern life. Onstage, a nude woman in a bathtub sings about the pleasures of hot running water.

*A NUMBERED GRAPH THAT SHOWS HOW EACH PART OF THE BODY WOULD FIT INTO A CHAIR:* Assorted papers related to Bauhaus designers, 1919–1984: Bauhaus Konvolut, design for a seat which accommodates a man 170 cm. tall. Pencil drawing which shows with a numbered graph how each part of the body would fit into a chair.

*THE HUMAN FIGURE IN A DRESS:* Oskar Schlemmer, *Triadic Ballet (Triadisches Ballett)*, 1922; Oskar Schlemmer, *Highly Simplified Head Construction (Profile) (Einfache Kopjkonstruktion [Profil])*, pencil and ink, 1928, Bühnen-Archiv.

*OUR GAME. OUR PARTY. OUR WORK.:* "Our Game. Our Party. Our Work." was the title of a lecture given by Johannes Itten, master teacher of the "preliminary course," upon his arrival at the Bauhaus in 1919. Rudolf Lutz designed a poster for the event.

*PORTRAIT IN THE FORM OF EPHEMERA:* Black and white photograph of Alan Turing, on the steps of the bus, with members of the Walton Athletic Club, 1946 (www.turing.org.uk). Article by Lucia Moholy, "The ASLIB Microfilm Service: The Story of Its Wartime Activities," *Journal of Documentation 2* (December 1946): 148–51.

*PHOTOGRAPH PRINTED WITH HATCH-MARKS OR LINES ACROSS THE PORTRAIT:* Getty Research Institute: Inventory of Bauhaus Student Work 1919–1933: Lotte Beese, ca. 1928, photograph of Xanti Schawinsky printed with hatch-marks or lines across the portrait.

*SELF-PORTRAIT IN THE BATHROOM MIRROR:* Ilse Gropius, silver gelatin print ca. 1926–27, Bauhaus-Archiv Berlin.

*IN THE GARDEN BEHIND THE MASTER'S HOUSE:* László Moholy-Nagy, photograph of Lucia Moholy, ca. 1925.

*IN THIS PHOTOGRAPH I AM UNTITLED:* Lucia Moholy, Self-portrait, silver gelatin print, 1931.

*THE DOLL SONG:* A song from *The Tales of Hoffman (Les Contes d'Hoffmann)*, an opera by Jacques Offenbach, based on three short stories by Ernst Theodore Wilhelm Hoffmann, pen name E.T.A., staged at the Kroll Opera House in Berlin (*Krolloper de Berlin*). László Moholy-Nagy designed the sets for Hoffmann's *Erzählungen* in 1929 and for *Madame Butterfly* in 1931. Lucia Moholy filmed the sets. From 1933 to 1942, the building housed the government of the German Reichstag. It was bombed by the Allies during WWII and finally demolished in 1951.

*STAIRWAY, SEASIDE:* László Moholy-Nagy, *Stairway in the Bexhill Seaside Pavillion* (Sussex, England), silver gelatin print, 1936. Karla Grosch (1904–1933), a trained dancer and one of only two female teachers at the Bauhaus in Dessau, taught gymnatics there from 1928 to 1932. In 1929, she performed in Oskar Schlemmer's *Glass Dance* and in *Metal Dance*. In a letter to Max Werner Lenz, an actor with whom she had an affair, Grosch wrote, ". . . this is the way I am, light-dark, warm-cold, up-down." In 1933, pregnant with Lenz's child, she immigrated to Palestine with a Bauhaus student and architect, Franz (Bobby) Aichinger. In Tel Aviv, in May of that year, she died of a heart attack while swimming in the sea.

*THE GAME OF ROLES:* The title of Luigi Pirandello's *The Game of Roles* (*Il giuoco delle parti*) is usually mistranslated into English as *The Rules of the Game*. The play was first performed in 1918. The characters in Pirandello's play, *Six Characters in Search of an Author* (*Sei personaggi in cerca d'autore*), are rehearsing this play. These two plays, plus *Tonight, We Improvise* (*Questa sera si recita a soggetto*) form a trilogy. The actors in Xanti Schawinsky's non-narrative "spectodrama" titled *Play, Life, Illusion* (1936–1937) are rehearsing *Tonight, We Improvise*. In an article in *The Drama Review* 15 (no. 3, Summer 1971), Schawinsky wrote that the rehearsal scene is one "in which a clashing encounter, reality and illusion, create staggering confusion" (quoted in *Xanti Schawinsky: Head Drawings and Faces of War*, The Drawing Center, 2014).

FRAGMENT OF A BRIDE: Grete Stern and Ellen (Rosenberg) Auerbach, silver gelatin print, 1930. In 1929, Stern and Auerbach opened an advertising studio under the name "ringl+pit," said to be their childhood nicknames.

GESTURE DANCE DIAGRAM: Oskar Schlemmer, sketch, 1926. *Gesture Dance* was one of several dances that grew out of Schlemmer's 1922 *Triadic Ballet*. The others were *Form Dance*, *Space Dance*, *Scenery Dance*, and *Hoop Dance*.

THE HEAD OF A DANCER: Lotte Jacobi, photograph of Niura Norskaya, silver gelatin print, 1929.

THE TRANSFORMATION ANXIETY DREAM: László Moholy-Nagy, *The Transformation/Anxiety Dream*, fotoplastique, 1925.

THE BRACELET: László Moholy-Nagy, bracelet, steel and plastic, n.d.

A BALLET BASED ON THE NUMBER THREE: Oskar Schlemmer's *Triadic Ballet* (*Triadisches Ballett*), which premiered in 1922, had three acts, each associated with a different color; three dancers (two male, one female); twelve dances; and eighteen costumes.

THE SHATTERED MARRIAGE: László Moholy-Nagy, *The Broken Marriage* (*Die zerrüttete ehe*), sometimes translated as *A Marriage Gone to Pieces*, fotoplastique, 1925.

ME, A CHRONICLE: Marianne Brandt, *me (Metal Workshop) in 9 years of the Bauhaus. a chronicle* (*me [Metallwerkstatt] in 9 jahre Bauhaus. eine chronik*), 1928, photomontage of silver gelatin prints on white cardboard.

THE POSSESSIVE FORM: Based on a Lucia Moholy resume found in the Lucia Moholy collection at the Bauhaus-Archiv Berlin.

*THE SCURRYING WHITE MICE DISAPPEAR:* Robert Walser, in "A Schoolboy's Diary and Other Stories" in *Fritz Kocher's Essays* (pub. 1904), translated by Damion Searls, New York Review Books, 2013, p. 17: "It is as though you could hear thought itself softly whispering, softly stirring. It's like the scurrying of little white mice."

*THINGS TO COME:* A 1936 film adapted by H. G. Wells from *The Shape of Things to Come*, his 1933 sci-fi novel. Ninety seconds of uncredited Moholy-Nagy designs are incorporated into the film.

*SHE HE AT THE FLOWER BASKET:* Matilde (Til) Brugman's "she he" (1917–1922) is a poem in French and English in which the word *Houbigant* appears. Houbigant Parfum was founded in Paris in 1775. The original shop was called *A la Corbeille de Fleurs* (At the Flower Basket). The title gestures to the fact that most flowers are bisexual. Those which are, are considered "perfect" since they have both male (*androecium*) and female (*gynoecium*) reproductive structures, i.e., male stamens and female ovaries. Lilies, roses, and most plants with large showy flowers are bisexual. This corresponds in psychology to the Jungian notion that there are female elements (anima) in every male psyche and male elements (*animus*) in every female.

*LONG-EXPOSURE PHOTOGRAPH OF A MAN:* Getty Research Institute: Inventory of Bauhaus Student Work 1919–1933: Unidentified student, ca. 1922, 1 double-exposed or long-exposure photograph of a man sitting in a Breuer chair.

*PORTRAIT AS SELF-PORTRAIT:* Lucia Moholy, portrait of László Moholy-Nagy, silver gelatin print, 1925.

*LAST NAME FIRST FIRST NAME LAST:* Based on multiple resumes found in the Lucia Moholy collection at the Bauhaus-Archiv Berlin.

*THE PHOTOGRAPHER, BERLIN:* Marianne Breslauer, silver gelatin print, 1933.

*THE NEW OBJECTIVITY:* Irene Bayer-Hecht and Herbert Bayer, *Costume for the "New Objectivity" Party (Figurine für das Fest "Neue Sachlichkeit")*, 1925.

*THE ICON IN THE HANDS OF THE ENEMY:* "Icon in the hands of the enemy: The Nazi party's school for administrators, ca. 1938," photo caption in *The Bauhaus Building in Dessau*, Spector Books, p. 112.

*ONE PHOTOGRAPH OF A ROOFTOP:* Getty Research Institute: Inventory of Bauhaus Student Work 1919–1933: Lucia Moholy-Nagy, 1931, 1 photograph of a rooftop.

*MASTERS' HOUSES:* Lucia Moholy, Double House Northwest Side (Kandinsky-Klee), silver gelatin print, 1926 / Walter Gropius (architect), Bauhaus-Archiv Berlin.

*TOMB IN THREE PARTS:* Paul Klee, watercolor and graphite on paper, 1923.

*THE EXPRESSION OF EMOTIONS: The Expression of Emotions in Man and Animals: With Photographic and Other Illustrations* is a book written by Charles Darwin and published in 1899 by D. Appleton and Company, New York. *The Disintegration Loops* is a series of four albums by American avant-garde composer William Basinski. The albums are a record of his attempt to transfer earlier recordings of "easy-listening" radio music, which had been made on magnetic tape, to a digital recorder. The tape, however, slowly deteriorated, creating a haunting sound that in time becomes elegiac. The recording coincidentally finished on 9/11/2001.

*MASK PHOTO:* Gertrude Arndt was a student in the weaving workshop from 1923 to 1927. In 1930, she produced a series of forty-three "mask portraits" (self-portraits in costume). Today her work is seen as anticipating Cindy Sherman's film still series. "You just need to open your eyes and already you are someone else, or you can open your mouth wide or something like that, and a different person has already appeared. And if you dress up in costume as well . . . It's like looking into the mirror and making faces . . . Basically a mirror image."—Gertrude Arndt on her "Mask Portraits" (http://bauhaus-online.de/en/atlas/werke/mask-portrait)

*AN ANATOMICAL STUDY:* Getty Research Institute: Inventory of Bauhaus Student Work 1919–1933: Erich Mrozek, n.d., 1 drawing of anatomical studies, possibly for Oskar Schlemmer's course "Man."

*THE MISSING NEGATIVES:* "The Missing Negatives" is the title of an essay written by Lucia Moholy and published in 1983 in the *British Journal of Photography*, 130 (7.1), pp 6–8, 18. The essay covers the unauthorized and unattributed use of her negatives by Walter Gropius during the war years and her legal efforts to have the negatives returned to her after the war.

*HAVING BOTH THE PRESENT AND FUTURE IN MIND:* Implosion of the Pruitt-Igoe housing project, St. Louis, Missouri, 1972, black and white photograph, Lee Balterman. The architectural critic Charles Jencks, in his 1977 book *The Language of Post-Modern Architecture*, called the demolition of the Pruitt-Igoe housing project, built in 1951–1955 by architect Minoru Yamasaki, "the death of Modern Architecture." Katharine Bristol, in an article titled "The Pruitt-Igoe Myth," published in 1991 in the *Journal of Architectural Education*: "By continuing to promote architectural solutions to what are fundamentally problems of class and race, the myth conceals the complete inadeuqacy of contemporary public housing policy." In *Marginal Notes* (55), Lucia Moholy writes of László Moholy-Nagy, "He always had the present and future in mind, hardly ever looking back to the historical past . . ."

## DISCLAIMER

While this book draws on historical research, it is a work of poetic fiction. Names, characters, places, events, and incidents outside the Notes section are either the products of the author's imagination or used in a fictitious manner. Any resemblance to actual persons, living or dead, or actual events is purely coincidental.

"When I state myself, as the representative of the verse, it does not mean me, but a supposed person." — Emily Dickinson (in a letter to Thomas Wentworth Higginson, dated July, 1862)

## ACKNOWLEDGMENTS

Thanks to the librarians at the Getty Research Institute in L.A. More thanks to Dr. Annemarie Jaeggi, Director of the Bauhaus, and her staff at the Library and Archive at the Bauhaus-Archiv in Berlin. Thanks also to Gahl Hodges Burt and Christine Wallich and the staff and Board of Trustees at the American Academy in Berlin for a 2015 Ellen Maria Gorrissen Fellowship that allowed me to spend time at the Bauhaus-Archiv in Berlin where the papers and photographs of Lucia Moholy and other Bauhaus women photographers are housed. Thanks to the fellows at the Academy for their interest in my project. Thanks to Dr. Rolf Sachsse, biographer of Lucia Moholy, for sharing with me his knowledge of Lucia Moholy and the Bauhaus community. Thanks to Emily Pulitzer and the Pulitzer Foundation where I first saw Lucia Moholy's photograph *Walter and Ilse Gropius's Dressing Room* displayed during the exhibition *In the Still Epiphany*. Seeing that image sparked my interest in Lucia Moholy and in the Bauhaus school and movement. That interest in time became an obsession, the final result of which is this book of poems.

Special thanks to book artist Ken Botnick for designing and publishing a limited edition artist's book of twenty-six poems from the manuscript, published by Emdash Design Studio under the title *The Illusion of Physicality*. Additional thanks are due for his design of the interior of *A Doll for Throwing*. Continued deeply affectionate thanks to Bill Clegg, and to Jeff Shotts, Fiona McCrae, and everyone at Graywolf Press who helped to produce this book. And thanks of the sort for which words are inadequate to friends and colleagues for their steadfast support and affection, especially Mark Bibbins, Timothy Donnelly, Jennifer Kronovet, Lynn Melnick, David Schuman, and Monica de la Torre (among many others who go unnamed here). Thanks to the Poetry Foundation for featuring the poem "Two Nudes" on poetrynow, a partnership between the Poetry Foundation and WFMT radio.

Thanks also to the editors of the following magazines and anthologies where individual poems appeared: *The Berlin Journal:* ONE GLASS NEGATIVE, SELF-PORTRAIT AS A PHOTOGRAPH OF A PLATTER, and ME, A CHRONICLE; *The Best American Poetry 2017*, David Lehman and Natasha Trethewey, eds, Scribner: ADMISSION; *Between the Breath and the Abyss: Poetics about Beauty* (bilingual anthology), Keila Vall, ed, Editorial Ígneo: THE DOLL SONG; *BOMB:* THE GAME OF ROLES, A BALLET BASED ON THE NUMBER THREE, THE EXPRESSION OF EMOTIONS, and THE MISSING NEGATIVES; *Poems for Political Disaster,* Timothy Donnelly, Barbara Fischer, Stefania Heim, eds, *Boston Review Chapbook:* IN NOVEMBER WE INCHED CLOSER; *February, an Anthology,* Paul Legault et. al., eds: THE MIRROR; *Granta* (online): A NUMBERED GRAPH THAT SHOWS HOW EACH PART OF THE BODY WOULD FIT INTO A CHAIR; *Liberation: New Works on Freedom,* Mark Ludwig, ed, Beacon Press: ONE PHOTOGRAPH OF A ROOFTOP; *The New Yorker:* HAVING BOTH THE PRESENT AND FUTURE IN MIND and THE HEAD OF A DANCER; *Oversound:* A MODEL OF A MACHINE, NEWS OF THE DAY, and IN THIS PHOTOGRAPH I AM UNTITLED; *The Paris Review:* ADMISSION, AN ANATOMI- CAL STUDY, SELF-PORTRAIT IN THE BATHROOM MIRROR, and IN THE GARDEN BEHIND THE MASTER'S HOUSE; *Poetry:* PORTRAIT IN THE FORM OF EPHEMERA and THE HUMAN FIGURE IN A DRESS; The Poetry Foundation Website: TWO NUDES; *Still Life with Poem: 100 Natures Mortes in Verse,* Jehanne Dubrow and Lindsay Lusby, eds, Literary House Press: THE BRACELET; *T Magazine, The New York Times:* LONG-EXPOSURE PHOTOGRAPH OF A MAN; *Tupelo Quarterly:* MASK PHOTO, THE TRANSFORMATION ANXIETY DREAM, TOMB IN THREE PARTS, and OUR GAME. OUR PARTY. OUR WORK.; *Vallum:* THE SCURRYING WHITE MICE DISAPPEAR.

STILL LIFE WITH GLASSES is for Hiroaki Sato (with thanks to and for the late Shuzo Takiguchi who brought us together). THE EXPRESSION OF EMOTIONS is for Barbara Elliot Martin. GESTURE DANCE DIAGRAM is for Ken Botnick.

**MARY JO BANG** is the author of seven previous poetry collections, including *The Last Two Seconds* and *Elegy*, winner of the National Book Critics Circle Award and a *New York Times* Notable Book. She has also published an acclaimed translation of Dante's *Inferno*. Bang has received a fellowship from the Guggenheim Foundation, a Hodder Fellowship from Princeton University, and a Berlin Prize Fellowship from the American Academy in Berlin. She is a professor of English and teaches in the creative writing program at Washington University in Saint Louis.

The text of *A Doll for Throwing* is set in ITC Franklin Gothic Book, original design by Morris Fuller Benton, 1902. Titles are Druk Text Medium Italic, designed by Berton Hasebe at Commercial Type Foundry, 2012. Design and composition by Ken Botnick at Emdash Design Studio, Saint Louis, Missouri. Manufactured by Versa Press on acid-free, 30 percent postconsumer wastepaper.